2020

A GIFT FOR:

Nana

FROM:

Jack + Drew

Published by Hallmark Gift Books,
a division of Hallmark Cards, Inc.,
Kansas City, MO 64141
Visit us on the Web at Hallmark.com.

Editorial Director: Delia Berrigan
Editor: Kara Goodier
Art Director: Chris Opheim
Designer: Brian Pilachowski
Production Designer: Dan Horton
Written by Keely Chace and Jeannie Hund

ISBN: 978-1-63059-677-4
BOK1503

Made in China
1118

BECAUSE SHE'S
NANA

Hallmark

THE BEST
AND
sweetest
ADVENTURES
BEGIN WITH
Nana.

SHE
LISTENS,
NOT ONLY WITH
HER EARS,
BUT WITH
HER WHOLE
heart.

IT'S A TECHNIQUE
SHE'S PERFECTED
OVER TIME.

BECAUSE SHE'S
Nana.

SHE BELIEVES IN
GOOD MANNERS,
GOOD MEALS,
LONG TALKS,
AND BIG

hugs.

NOT NECESSARILY
IN THAT ORDER.

HER CASA ES
SU CASA.
HER COUCH IS
YOUR COUCH.
HER SNACKS ARE
YOUR SNACKS.

BECAUSE SHE'S
Nana.

SHE'S A WORK OF
heart.

SHE'S
Nana.

SHE BRINGS OUT THE

goodness

IN EVERYONE . . .

PROBABLY
BECAUSE THERE'S
SO MUCH OF IT
IN HER.

EVERYONE IS
DRAWN TO HER
WARM, CARING VIBE.

BECAUSE IT'S PURE
Nana.

SHE CAN
TURN A WHOLE
DAY AROUND
WITH ALL THE SKILL
OF A LONGTIME TRUCKER
BACKING A
FIFTY-FOOT TRAILER.

SHE GIVES
THE GENTLEST
AND SMARTEST ADVICE—

THE KIND
THAT SEEMS EVEN
WISER
EACH TIME YOU REVISIT IT—
BECAUSE SHE'S
LIVED IT AND
EARNED IT.

AND BECAUSE SHE'S
Nana.

AND SPEAKS FROM HER *heart* ALWAYS.

SMILES
HAPPEN.
RULES
ARE STRETCED.
BEDTIMES
HAVE WIGGLE ROOM.

BECAUSE
Nana's
IN THE HOUSE.

SHE'S LIKE THE SPARKLING WATER OF PEOPLE—

bubbly
AND
fun.

HER FAVORITE
WORD IS
yes.

BECAUSE
GOOD THINGS
HAPPEN TO THOSE
WHO ASK
Nana.

GRANDKIDS
TAKE UP A
BIG SPACE
IN HER
heart ...

AND THEY'RE *welcome* TO IT.

YOU'LL OUTGROW
HER LAP,
BUT NEVER HER
heart.

BECAUSE SHE'S
Nana,
AND
HER HEART
GOES WITH YOU
EVERYWHERE.

SHE'S AN
angel,
BUT NOT ALL ANGEL.
NANA'S GOT
A HEALTHY
MISCHIEVOUS
STREAK.

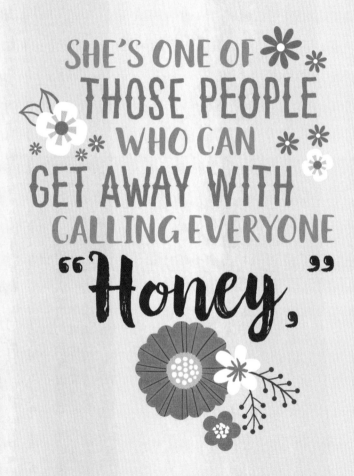

SHE'S ONE OF
THOSE PEOPLE
WHO CAN
GET AWAY WITH
CALLING EVERYONE
"Honey,"

BUT SHE MOSTLY RESERVES IT FOR FAMILY.

BECAUSE SHE'S *Nana.*

SHE SPOILS
YOU OUTRAGEOUSLY,
GIVES
SELFLESSLY,
AND
loves
UNCONDITIONALLY.

SHE TEACHES
THE MOST
IMPORTANT STUFF
WITHOUT
SAYING A WORD...

BECAUSE SHE'S
Nana.

There's no love

quite like her love.

THE WORLD IS A
SOFTER, HAPPIER PLACE...

BECAUSE

Nana
IS HERE.

She's style, class

& sass combined.

SHE.
TAKES CARE
OF BUSINESS
WITH A
smile
AND A
wink
(AND GETS 'EM TO
THROW IN EXTRAS).

HER **cookie jar** FLOWETH OVER— UNLESS YOU PREFER SALTY,

IN WHICH CASE, SHE'LL STAY WELL STOCKED ON *chips.*

BECAUSE SHE'S *Nana.*

There's no place

like Nana's.

BECAUSE
COOKIES
WON'T EAT THEMSELVES.
BECAUSE EXTRA
CARTOONS
MEAN EXTRA FUN.

BECAUSE
HUGS
ARE THE VERY
BEST VITAMINS.

THERE'S
Nana.

HER PHONE IS
FULL OF
PHOTOS.
HER HEART IS
FULL OF
LOVE.

SHE'S
Nana.

SHE ADMIRES YOUR
ACCOMPLISHMENTS
HOWEVER
BIG OR
SMALL.

SHE MAKES YOU
FEEL
happy
JUST TO BE YOU . . .

BECAUSE SHE'S
Nana.

AT HER HOUSE, THERE ARE
ALWAYS ENOUGH
dessert, laughs,
AND hugs.

SHE SEES
THE BEST
IN YOU,
EVEN WHEN
YOU FEEL
YOUR WORST.

BECAUSE NANA
IS NO FAIR-WEATHER FAN,
AND SHE
cheers
YOU ON, WIN OR LOSE.

SHE'LL LET
YOU KNOW
IF THAT SMALL STUFF
IS WORTH
SWEATING OR NOT.
She knows.

She's Nana.

SHE'S LIVED SOME PRETTY

wild stories.

BUT SHE'S NOT ABOVE
A LITTLE
EMBELLISHMENT
HERE AND THERE FOR
ENTERTAINMENT
VALUE.

SHE'S NEVER BELIEVED IN "light

efreshments."

BECAUSE SHE'S

Nana.

SHE'LL MAKE YOUR DAY.
OR YOUR WEEK.
OR YOUR MONTH.
OR WHATEVER LENGTH
OF TIME YOU NEED.

BECAUSE SHE'S

Nana.

FREE WITH
HUGS.
GENEROUS WITH
LAUGHTER.
SHINING WITH
LOVE.

THAT'S Nana FOR YOU.

TOGETHER IS HER
FAVORITE PLACE
TO BE.

loves even more.

THAT'S HOW SHE BECAME

Nana.

If you enjoyed this book
or it has touched your life in some way,
we'd love to hear from you.

Please write a review at Hallmark.com,
e-mail us at booknotes@hallmark.com,
or send your comments to:

Hallmark Book Feedback
P.O. Box 419034
Mail Drop 100
Kansas City, MO 64141